IF YOU WERE THERE

BIBLICAL TIMES

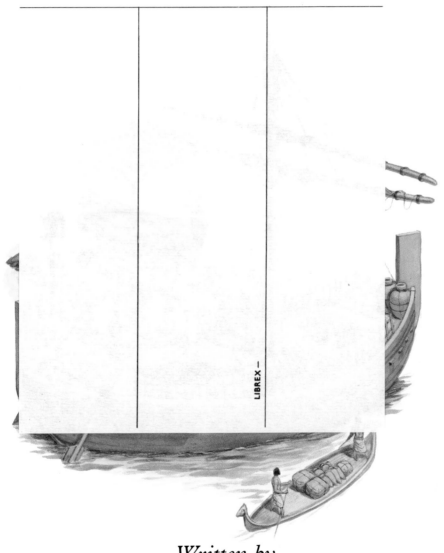

Written by
Antony Mason

MARSHALL PUBLISHING • LONDON

CONTENTS

INTRODUCTION

The Bible lands occupy the eastern end of the Mediterranean Sea. Unlike Egypt or Mesopotamia, they were neither the setting for any great early civilisations nor at the centre of any splendid ancient empires. The events that took place there were barely noticed by the major civilisations of the day. Yet their effect on world history has been huge. The story of the people who lived here forms an essential part of two of the great religions of the world – Judaism and Christianity.

Their story is found in the books of the Bible. Although the Bible was written in ancient times, often long after the events described, much of it turns out to be true history. This has been confirmed by archaeological discoveries and ancient records found in Egypt, Mesopotamia and in the Bible lands themselves. Over the years it has become possible to uncover the real historical events that lie behind the stories in the Bible, and to learn how the people of the Bible lands really lived.

THE FIRST CIVILISATIONS

A lyre with a bull's head, from Ur

According to the Bible, Abraham left the city of Ur in Mesopotamia in about 1800 B.C. and travelled to the green and fertile land of Canaan. By this time the two great civilisations of the fertile crescent, Egypt and Mesopotamia, had been in existence for well over 1,000 years. Many Canaanites lived and worked in northern Egypt. Joseph, the great-grandson of Abraham, joined them when his brothers sold him into slavery. Later, as a powerful officer in the court of the pharaoh (the king of Egypt), he brought his 11 brothers to Egypt, and they founded the 12 tribes of Israel.

The Israelites became virtual slaves to the Egyptians, until they were driven out in about 1300 B.C.

The fertile crescent

The two ancient civilisations of Egypt and Mesopotamia, and the region between them, have been called the "fertile crescent" because of the richness of the land. Ancient Egypt developed on the banks of the Nile. Mesopotamia lay between the Tigris and Euphrates rivers. Canaan lay between these two great civilisations.

The columns supporting the roof were decorated with paintings and carvings and the Egyptian form of picture-writing known as hieroglyphics. Some of the pictures and writing tell the story of real historical events.

▲The Egyptians built some of the greatest buildings of the ancient world. Many of these were temples to their gods. It is thought that Canaanites living in Egypt at that time may have been forced to work on the construction sites.

Cyprus

Mediterranean Sea

FERTILE CRESCENT

Mesopotamia

Tigris

Euphrates

Canaan

Egypt

Persian Gulf

Nile River

Red Sea

Shrine

Gatehouse

Central stairway

Terraces

Walls made of mud bricks

The ziggurat

Vast, towerlike temples, called ziggurats, rose up from the middle of many of the cities in Mesopotamia. These were built on mounds, like stepped pyramids. They had very few rooms inside. Outside stairs led up to the shrine on the top, where the gods were said to come down from heaven to visit the earth. Sacrifices and offerings to the gods were made at the shrine, while ceremonies and processions took place in the open air on the terraces.

The inside of some Egyptian temples was like a forest of closely packed columns, rising to heights of 15 metres or more.

Egyptian clothing was very simple. Men wore loincloths made of linen, a material woven from the fibres of flax plants. Priests, like this man, and priestesses wore more elaborate robes.

ANCIENT TOYS

Many objects from daily life have been found in tombs in Mesopotamia and Egypt. Among them are toys, such as dolls, spinning tops and wooden animals. Clearly, people living 5,000 years ago enjoyed games as much as we do today.

NOMADS IN A HARSH LAND

After leaving Egypt, the Israelites wandered through the dry lands to the south of Canaan. They passed through the rocky mountains of the Sinai Peninsula, where God gave their leader, Moses, the Ten Commandments. Later they moved into the Negev Desert and then to the east of the River Jordan.

A water bag made from a goat skin

Most of these lands are desert and there is not enough rainfall throughout the year to grow crops. However, water can be found at oases. It is possible to live in these harsh lands by herding animals, such as goats and camels. But the herders have to live as nomads, constantly moving their tents in search of new pastures. This is how many of the Bedouin people of the Middle East still live today.

Water was extremely precious in the desert. Permanent water supplies could be found only at oases. Some of these were spots in the desert where water bubbled out as a spring. Underground water could also be reached by a well.

A world of cloth

As nomadic herders, the Israelites would have had very few possessions. Everything had to be packed in small bundles to put on the back of a camel or donkey. Their clothes, rugs and tents were all made of cloth, which they wove themselves on simple wooden looms. Stones were attached to the ends of the vertical threads to keep them taut.

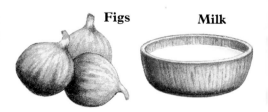

The tents were made out of strips of woven goat hair about a metre wide. These were sewn together and propped up on wooden poles.

DESERT FOOD

Animals provided the nomads with meat and milk from which cheese and yoghurt could be made. Using flour bought from farmers, they could bake flat sheets of unleavened bread, made without yeast. Figs and dates came from oasis trees.

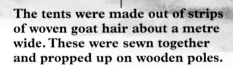

Figs

Milk

The ship of the desert

When humans learned how to use camels more than 3,000 years ago, life in the desert became much easier. Camels can travel for as long as two weeks without any water and they can carry heavy loads. Because of this, the Arabs have called them "the ships of the desert". Camels also provide milk, meat and hair for cloth.

Shepherds had to guard their flocks against attacks by lions, leopards, wolves and hyenas.

◀ *In the heat of the day, children sheltered in the shade of the tent. But during the rest of the day they had to work. The boys helped to herd the animals and the girls helped to grind flour, cook and spin thread for weaving into cloth.*

There was little furniture in a tent. The nomads sat and slept on rugs spread on the ground.

▼ *The landscape to the east of the River Jordan and the Dead Sea (below) is probably even drier now than it was when the Israelites wandered through it with their herds.*

Dates

Goat meat

Unleavened bread

THE PROMISED LAND

Cucumber

Olives

Pomegranate

From the rocky Judean hills the Israelites could look down upon the green valleys of Canaan. The Canaanites were not nomads. They were farmers who worked the land and lived in permanent villages made up of clusters of small, mud-brick houses. Some of the world's oldest farming communities developed in Canaan as long ago as 8,000 B.C.

Wheat grain

Several of these villages grew into cities, such as Jerusalem, Jericho, and Hazor which had a population of 20,000.

According to the Bible stories about Canaan, Abraham had been promised these lands of "milk and honey" by God.

▲ *The main crop of Canaan was wheat. But farmers also grew a wide variety of fruits and vegetables, such as figs, apples, melons, leeks, onions, garlic and lentils. They made wine and raisins from grapes and oil from olives.*

Men and women wore tunics made of wool or linen and sandals made of leather.

▲ *Ploughing took place after the first rains in October. Ploughs drawn by animals, such as donkeys (above), are still in use today, although many farmers use tractors.*

Grain which fell during harvesting was carefully collected, or "gleaned", by the women.

The seasons

Like farmers all over the world, the Canaanites followed a pattern of work that was ruled by the seasons. Seeds were sown during the winter rainy season. Barley was harvested in April, then the wheat. The grapes ripened during the dry season and were picked in August. Dates and figs were ready in September.

January February March April May June July August September October November December

The house

Mud bricks make a good building material in a dry climate. The bricks are made of slabs of mud mixed with straw and dried in the sun. The houses usually consisted of two floors. The flat roof was used to dry grain, raisins and figs, and was used as an outdoor room in the hot summer. The family used the roof for sleeping in hot weather, but they slept on the first floor in the winter. They had little furniture and few possessions.

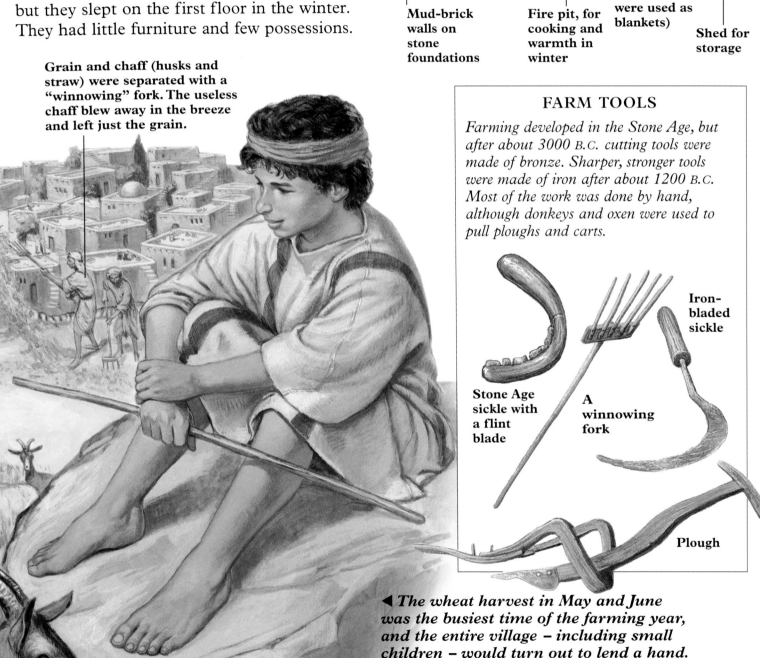

Mud-brick walls on stone foundations

Fire pit, for cooking and warmth in winter

Sleeping mat (woollen cloaks were used as blankets)

Shed for storage

Grain and chaff (husks and straw) were separated with a "winnowing" fork. The useless chaff blew away in the breeze and left just the grain.

FARM TOOLS

Farming developed in the Stone Age, but after about 3000 B.C. cutting tools were made of bronze. Sharper, stronger tools were made of iron after about 1200 B.C. Most of the work was done by hand, although donkeys and oxen were used to pull ploughs and carts.

Stone Age sickle with a flint blade

A winnowing fork

Iron-bladed sickle

Plough

◀ *The wheat harvest in May and June was the busiest time of the farming year, and the entire village – including small children – would turn out to lend a hand. Canaanites also raised herds of goats and sheep, and it was often the job of the young boys to look after the animals.*

11

KINGS AND CITIES

The Egyptians held Canaan until about 1150 B.C. When they left, the Israelites took over the land and divided it up between the 12 tribes of Israel. Bible stories tell us how the Israelites appointed a king, Saul, to lead them against their rivals, the Philistines, and how David helped Saul defeat them.
When Saul died, David was proclaimed king. He captured Jerusalem and made it his capital.

According to the Bible, David united the Israelites in a single kingdom that covered the whole of Canaan and beyond. After the reign of David's son, Solomon, ended in 928 B.C., the kingdom split into two – Israel in the north, with its capital at Samaria, and Judah (or Judea) in the south, with its capital at Jerusalem.

Canaanite pottery jugs

The Philistines

In about 1250 B.C. the Philistines, who were part of the group known as the "Sea People", moved into the Bible lands from the northern Mediterranean, and settled in the fertile coastal region in the south of Canaan. By about 1020 B.C. they were beginning to take over the lands of the Israelite tribes, but under David they were pushed back toward the coasts. Foreign conquerors destroyed the Philistines in the 6th century B.C., but the name lives on – Philistine is the origin of the word "Palestine".

A Philistine soldier

The cities were built on hilltops and protected by high walls.

▶ *Since its capture by David 3,000 years ago, Jerusalem (right) has become a sacred city for three major religions: Judaism, Christianity and Islam. The Dome of the Rock, built in A.D. 961, is believed to mark the spot where Muhammad ascended to paradise.*

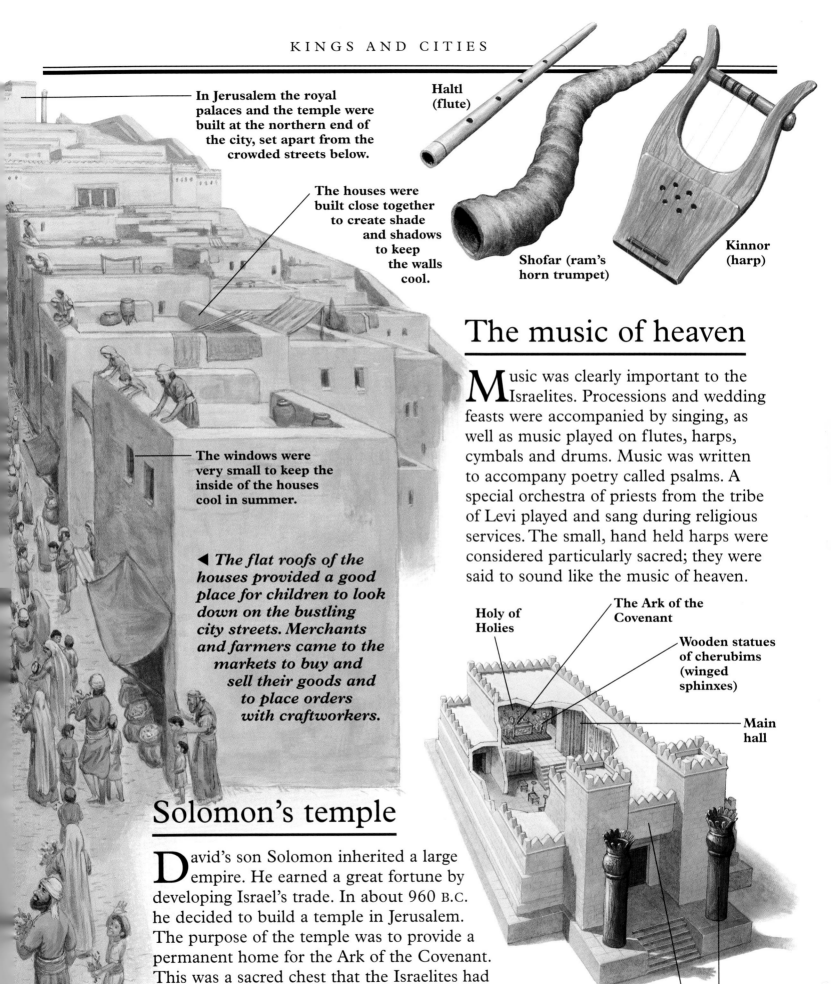

In Jerusalem the royal palaces and the temple were built at the northern end of the city, set apart from the crowded streets below.

Haltl (flute)

Shofar (ram's horn trumpet)

Kinnor (harp)

The houses were built close together to create shade and shadows to keep the walls cool.

The windows were very small to keep the inside of the houses cool in summer.

◄ *The flat roofs of the houses provided a good place for children to look down on the bustling city streets. Merchants and farmers came to the markets to buy and sell their goods and to place orders with craftworkers.*

The music of heaven

Music was clearly important to the Israelites. Processions and wedding feasts were accompanied by singing, as well as music played on flutes, harps, cymbals and drums. Music was written to accompany poetry called psalms. A special orchestra of priests from the tribe of Levi played and sang during religious services. The small, hand held harps were considered particularly sacred; they were said to sound like the music of heaven.

Holy of Holies

The Ark of the Covenant

Wooden statues of cherubims (winged sphinxes)

Main hall

Solomon's temple

David's son Solomon inherited a large empire. He earned a great fortune by developing Israel's trade. In about 960 B.C. he decided to build a temple in Jerusalem. The purpose of the temple was to provide a permanent home for the Ark of the Covenant. This was a sacred chest that the Israelites had brought with them from the desert. It contained the stone tablets of the Ten Commandments.

Porch

Brass pillar

THE PHOENICIANS

The inside of King Solomon's temple was lined with wood from the cedars of Lebanon. This wood was one of the main goods traded by the Phoenicians, seafaring people who occupied the area of what is now modern day Lebanon. They lived in independent coastal cities, such as Tyre, Sidon and Beirut. Phoenicia was at the centre of a web of trading routes between Egypt, Mesopotamia and the civilisations of the Mediterranean, such as the Minoans on the island of Crete and the Mycenaeans in Greece. Trade went by sea, but also followed the caravan routes through Judah and Israel and along the path of the Fertile Crescent.

The Phoenicians were the greatest traders of the Mediterranean from about 1200 B.C. to 300 B.C.

An ivory carving

Phoenician purple

T he Phoenicians produced a purple cloth which became one of the most luxurious materials of the Mediterranean world. Later, the Romans declared that only their leaders could wear it. The dye was made from the murex sea snail. Some 60,000 shells were needed to produce just half a kilogram of dye, making the cloth very expensive. The Greek word for purple is *phoenix*, and this may be the origin of the name Phoenician.

The broad width of the ships made them stable and also allowed the merchants to fill them with huge cargoes of goods.

Murex shell

▲ *The Phoenicians built the best ships in the Mediterranean, and they were the most adventurous seafarers of their day. In about 600 B.C. the Egyptian pharaoh organised an expedition which apparently sailed all the way around Africa. This was not done again for nearly 2,000 years.*

To withstand rough seas, Phoenician trading ships were built of strong planks of cedar attached to a heavy wooden frame.

Pottery mask

Bronze calf

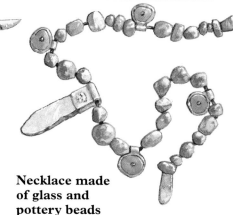

Necklace made of glass and pottery beads

Phoenician trading ships were slow and stable and they could be sailed by a crew of just three or four.

Running around the base of the hull was a heavy keel which made the ship more stable. These trading vessels became known as "round ships" because of their shape.

International trade

The Phoenicians traded in valuable goods from all over the Mediterranean region: cedar wood from Lebanon, ivory from Africa, pottery from Greece, wool from Turkey, jewels from Mesopotamia, tin from Spain, sheets of papyrus from Egypt and spices that had arrived overland from southern Asia. But they were not just traders; they were also gifted craftworkers, famous for their imaginative pottery and sculpture, jewellery and ivory carvings. They made beautiful glass, such as this colourfully decorated vase (right), from the fine sands of the Phoenician coast, and they were the first to learn how to make clear glass.

Glass vase

THE PHOENICIAN ALPHABET

The Mesopotamians wrote in cuneiform and the Egyptians used hieroglyphics. Both started out as picture-writing and used symbols to represent things or the sounds of words. The Phoenicians developed a much more efficient system of writing using an alphabet of just 22 letters that represented all the sounds of speech. The Greeks borrowed this to create their alphabet, and this developed into the alphabet we use today.

A B CG D E V(W)F H I K L M N P Q R S T O

WAR AND CONQUEST

The position of Israel, Judah and Phoenicia meant they were in the path of every conquering army that passed through the region. The Assyrians from northern Mesopotamia invaded Israel in 725 B.C. and captured Samaria. Jerusalem resisted Assyrian attacks, but was destroyed by the Babylonians of central Mesopotamia, who had conquered Judah in 597 B.C. About 5,000 Judeans (or Jews) were taken to Babylon as prisoners. The Babylonian captivity lasted almost 50 years, until Babylon was conquered by the Persians. The Persians allowed the Jews to return to their homeland. But, in turn, the Persians were defeated by Alexander the Great, who swept through the region in 334 B.C.

A Persian warrior in pottery tiles

▼ *The Assyrian army was powerful and well-trained – and greatly feared for its ruthless cruelty. Sieges were carried out mainly by spearmen, archers and slingsmen. A town was surrounded, starved of food and repeatedly attacked.*

Chariots formed an important part of the Assyrians' impressive forces. They were also used by the generals to enable them to travel about the battlefield quickly and direct operations.

Helmets and headdresses

The kings and soldiers of the ancient world can be identified by the distinctive headgear they wore. Helmets could do little more than offer some protection against glancing blows from swords, axes and clubs, but they made a warrior look more impressive and fearsome. The Philistines wore headdresses decorated with feathers, perhaps concealing a helmet. The Persians wore cylindrical helmets with long strips of metal at the sides and back to protect their cheeks and the back of the neck.

The attackers climbed the walls on ladders, protected by the fire of their own archers and slingsmen.

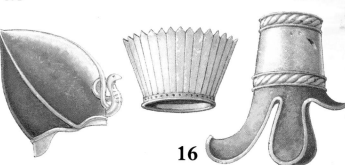

Assyrian   Egyptian war crown   Philistine   Persian

◀ *In Babylon, the splendid Ishtar Gate (left), decorated with ceramic dragons and bulls, led to the royal palace and a huge temple.*

Battering rams, protected by leather and wooden shields, were wheeled into position to knock down walls and city gates. Defenders would hurl flaming torches at them to try to set them alight.

Slings could kill at a distance of 90 metres – a longer range than most bows and arrows of the time.

Alexander the Great

When he was just 30 years old, Alexander the Great was master of the largest empire the ancient world had ever known, stretching from Greece to northern India. He had become king of Macedonia, a neighbour of Greece, at the age of 20. In 334 B.C. he set out to defeat the Persians, conquering Egypt on the way. He took over the Persian empire – including the Bible lands – in 331 B.C. He died in 323 B.C., at 33 years of age.

A bronze statue of Alexander the Great

WEAPONS

The Assyrians had strong, sharp weapons with iron tips and blades. The main weapons for hitting an enemy at a distance were bows and arrows, and slings, which fired small round stones. At close quarters, swords, daggers, clubs and axes were used.

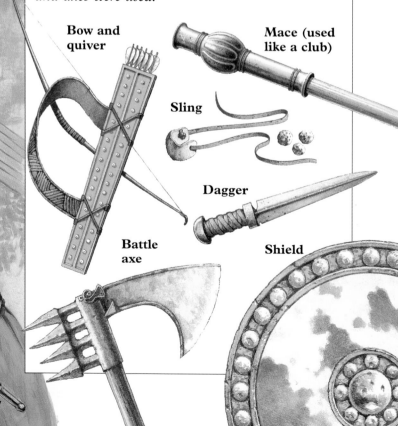

Bow and quiver

Mace (used like a club)

Sling

Dagger

Battle axe

Shield

RELIGIONS

A bull, one of the false Israelite gods

The Israelites had one God, and they believed that this God would protect them, provided that they were faithful to him alone. All around them were people who believed in a number of gods. In bad times, some Israelites were tempted to follow the gods of their neighbours, such as the Phoenicians. And when their lands were occupied by foreign powers, such as the Assyrians, Babylonians or Greeks, they adopted some of their gods. But these foreign gods were always condemned by their religious leaders and prophets. When the Persians allowed the Israelites to return to Jerusalem, they developed a much firmer idea of their own God and faith.

THE GODS OF EGYPT

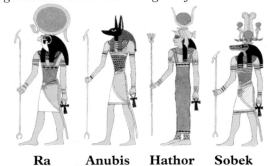

Many of the Egyptian gods were related to death and the after-life. The sun-god, Ra, was the most important. Anubis was the judge of the dead. Hathor was the sky goddess. Sobek was the god of crocodiles.

Ra   Anubis   Hathor   Sobek

Tombs and burials

Different religions had their own ideas about what happened after death and this affected how people were buried. The ancient Egyptians believed that the dead went to live in an afterworld where they needed their body and their possessions. This is why the bodies were preserved as mummies and buried in tombs filled with furniture, games, weapons and even food. The Canaanites and Israelites tended to put their dead in family tombs.

The tent contained the Ark of the Covenant and other sacred treasures.

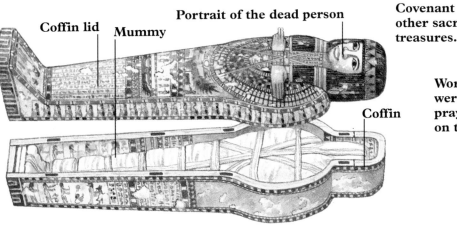

Coffin lid   Mummy   Portrait of the dead person

Coffin

Worshippers were called to prayer by blasts on the shofar.

Canaanite gods

To the Canaanites, the success of the crops was a matter of life and death, and this can be seen in the gods that they worshipped (right). The most powerful god was El, the sky god and creator of the world. His wife was Asherah, a mother goddess. They had a family of about 70 gods. The most important of these was Baal, the god of winter storms, who brought rain for the crops. Others include Astarte, goddess of fertility, and Rashef, the god of thunder and lightning.

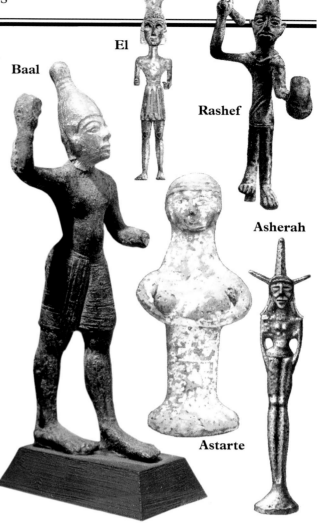

El

Baal

Rashef

Asherah

Astarte

On his chest the priest wore a large purse bearing 12 jewels, one for each of the tribes of Israel.

▲ *When the Israelites were still nomads, they held their religious ceremonies in the open air in front of a tent called the tabernacle. Animal sacrifice was an important part of all the religions at this time.*

Mesopotamian religion

There were hundreds of local gods in the cities of Mesopotamia, but the main gods show their worshippers' interests in the stars and sky and their concerns for agriculture and the forces of nature. In Sumer, An was the sky-god, Enki was the god of water and the sun-god was Uru. Both Babylonia and Assyria followed these gods, although they gave them different names. They also had their own local gods. In Babylonia, Marduk was important, and in Assyria it was Ashur (after whom Assyria was named).

A statue of a winged bull – the Assyrian guardian spirit that protected doorways.

HEROD'S JERUSALEM

People ate their food with their fingers, sometimes using pieces of bread to scoop up the sauce.

A Roman glass measuring cup

Following the death of Alexander the Great, his generals took control of the Bible lands. Later they tried to force the Jews to abandon their religion. The Jews revolted, and after about 20 years of struggle, Judah became a free kingdom again.

However, the great Roman empire had already begun to spread its control throughout the Mediterranean region and in 67 B.C. the Romans invaded Judah. They appointed their own supporters as rulers. One of these was Herod the Great, a cruel tyrant, who died in 4 B.C. It is believed this was the year that Jesus was born.

▶ *This Roman glass bottle from the first century A.D. is typical of the type of bottle that would have been used in Roman households.*

A Roman soldier

The Roman empire

Rome, in central Italy, was the home of the Romans. In about 250 B.C. they began to use their highly trained army to extend their power over neighbouring countries. They conquered Greece in 146 B.C. and had conquered most of western Europe by about 4 B.C. Shortly after Herod's death, they took direct control of the Bible lands, which they made into the Roman provinces of Judea and Samaria.

▲ *Wealthy Jews and others in the Bible lands often lived in splendid villas, where they held lavish dinner parties. Herod had turned Jerusalem into a wealthy and handsome city, with many features of other Roman cities, such as theatres and a stadium for chariot racing.*

Guests at dinner sat on chairs, although some may have preferred to lie on a couch, as the Romans did when they were eating.

Holy of Holies (the most holy part of the temple)

Sanctuary

Court of the priests

Nicanor Gate

Altar

Court of the Israelites

Court of the women

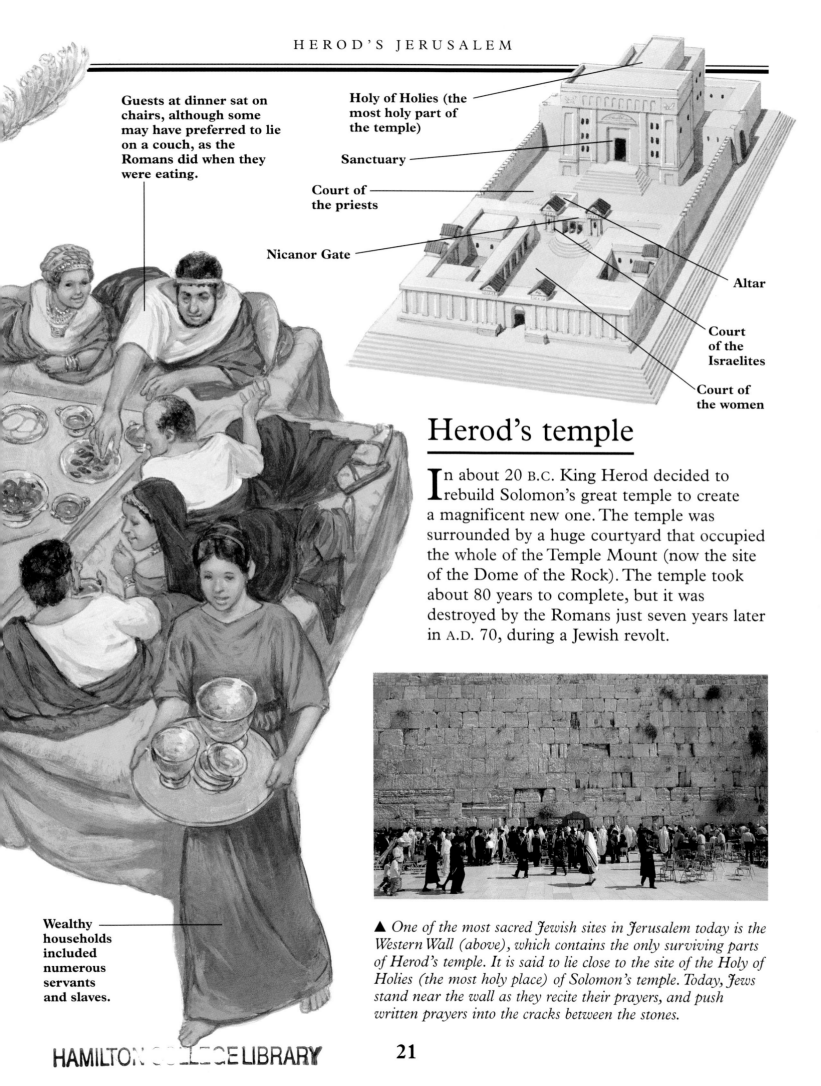

Wealthy households included numerous servants and slaves.

Herod's temple

In about 20 B.C. King Herod decided to rebuild Solomon's great temple to create a magnificent new one. The temple was surrounded by a huge courtyard that occupied the whole of the Temple Mount (now the site of the Dome of the Rock). The temple took about 80 years to complete, but it was destroyed by the Romans just seven years later in A.D. 70, during a Jewish revolt.

▲ One of the most sacred Jewish sites in Jerusalem today is the Western Wall (above), which contains the only surviving parts of Herod's temple. It is said to lie close to the site of the Holy of Holies (the most holy place) of Solomon's temple. Today, Jews stand near the wall as they recite their prayers, and push written prayers into the cracks between the stones.

CARPENTERS AND FISHERMEN

Pottery water jars

Herod's death led to a time of troubles in the Bible lands. The Jews disliked Herod's family, and they did not like being ruled by the Romans and paying taxes to them. It is believed that Jesus was born in Bethlehem because his parents had to go there and register to be taxed. The story of Jesus' birth tells us how he came from a humble and ordinary working family. When he was about 30 years old, he began his teaching. His fame spread fast, both as a teacher and as a healer. His teachings appealed especially to ordinary people – such as the farming families, craftworkers and fishing folk from Nazareth and Galilee – because he came from a similar background to them and understood their needs.

Money

Jesus said, "Pay to Caesar what is due to Caesar", referring to the Roman coins used by traders in the Bible lands. By the 20s and 30s A.D., coins were widely used for trading. Roman coins had a picture of the Roman ruler on them. But Jewish coins, such as *shekels*, were decorated with plants or different symbols because pictures of people were forbidden by Jewish law.

Jewish *shekel*

Roman coin

In Jesus' time there were hundreds of fishing boats on the Sea of Galilee. People still fish here today.

Learning a craft

Most craftworkers learned their skills as children, by spending their days helping their parents. At the age of about 15, they would know enough to set up in business on their own. Jesus probably helped his father in his carpenter's workshop. Carpenters made farm tools, such as ploughs, as well as furniture, doors and roof beams for houses. Other skilled workers included blacksmiths, potters and tanners (who made leather).

Traders and shopkeepers

Trade has been carried out in the same streets of the old city of Jerusalem for thousands of years. The city shops of Herod's times probably looked very much the same as they do now (left). These shops are often tiny and crammed with goods that are also displayed on tables on the pavement. Traders specialising in certain goods are often found side by side in the street.

The Sea of Galilee contained plenty of fish, which fishermen caught in nets cast from boats or from the shore.

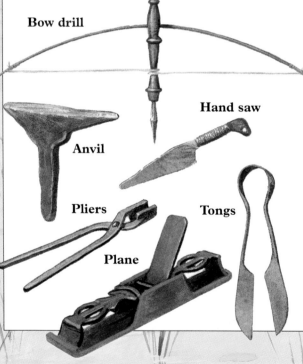

WORKING TOOLS

The tools that Jesus might have seen in his father's workshop had been developed over some 5,000 years. They were made of wood and iron – simple but strong. Many required the skills of a blacksmith. Beating hot iron on his anvil, he made tools such as shears for cutting the wool from sheep and the blades for carpenter's tools such as saws and planes.

Bow drill

Hand saw

Anvil

Pliers

Tongs

Plane

◀ *Many of Jesus' early meetings supposedly took place on the shores of the Sea of Galilee, where he healed the sick and performed various miracles. The Sea of Galilee is in fact a large freshwater lake, called Tiberias, on the River Jordan.*

BREAD OF HEAVEN

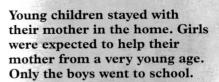

Food played an important part in the teaching of Jesus. Many of his parables are based on farming images. His first miracle took place at a marriage feast, when he turned water into fine wine.

For most people food was very simple, consisting mainly of bread, beans, vegetables and fruit. The women's main task at home was to prepare meals. The family would come together for a special supper on Friday evening. This was the beginning of the Sabbath, the Jewish day of rest, which lasted from sunset on Friday to sunset on Saturday. In poor families, meat was a rare luxury and was eaten only on special occasions and religious feast days.

Cheese, bread and chicken

▶ *Dried fruits, such as figs, dates and raisins, were eaten at the Passover festival. Dried figs were often pressed together to form a kind of cake.*

Olive oil was one of the main products of the Bible lands. It was stored in large, tall jars made of pottery.

Pressed fig cake

Young children stayed with their mother in the home. Girls were expected to help their mother from a very young age. Only the boys went to school.

The women had to bake bread every day. The bread dough was kneaded by hand.

Flour, water and yeast

Bread has always been an essential food in the Middle East. Grain was ground into flour using mills, and then mixed with water to make dough.

The rich ate wheat bread; the poor made their bread from barley. Some bread dough was allowed to rise so that the bread became spongy. But flat, "unleavened" (unrisen) bread was also made.

A hand operated mill for grinding grain at home

Oil lamps

Wick

Pottery lamp

Oil

In the Bible lands, people used small oil lamps to light their homes. They were usually made of pottery and burned olive oil. They gave off a dim light. People were used to the dark. They went to bed early and got up early to make full use of the daylight.

Small bread ovens were made of clay and were heated by burning wood in them.

Butter was made by swinging milk in a leather container. The fat separated from the milk to form the butter.

◀*Unleavened bread is still made in the Middle East today (left). Cooked on a flat, heated surface, the dough makes thin sheets of bread, rather like pitta bread. This bread has a special place in the Jewish religion and it was the kind of bread that Jesus shared with his apostles at the Last Supper.*

▲ *Women ran the home. They prepared the food and did the cooking. Most of these activities took place in the open courtyard in good weather. Although most houses contained just one family, all the relatives living nearby would remain in close contact.*
A woman could usually rely on the help of the other women of her family, especially her daughters.

KITCHEN UTENSILS

Containers and tools in the kitchen were usually very simple. Most bowls and plates were made of pottery, although wood was also used. The blades of sharp knives were made of iron. Bronze was used to make more expensive jugs and trays.

Drinking cup

Pottery jar

Wooden bowl

Iron knife

Bronze jug

Wooden plate

THE WORLD BEYOND

An early Christian symbol

It was during Passover in about A.D. 29 that Jesus was arrested just outside Jerusalem. He had upset many people with his teachings – the Jewish priests, the strict Jews and also the Romans, who were frightened that he would stir up trouble. Jesus was considered to be a rebel, and he was given the usual punishment for a rebel – death by crucifixion.

▲ *This coin commemorates the Romans' capture of Jerusalem and defeat of Judah during the First Jewish Revolt of A.D. 67–73.*

By this time the Bible lands formed part of the huge Roman empire, and before long, Jesus' message had begun to spread through it. But the Romans thought that Christianity was a dangerous way of thinking, and many early Christians were tortured and killed. It took 300 years for the Roman empire to become Christian.

Spreading the word

After Jesus' death, his close followers, the apostles, set about spreading his teachings, or "gospels". But it was the newcomer Paul who spread the word of Christ farthest. He made three great journeys through Roman lands, setting up numerous churches on the way.

Scribes wrote with a reed pen, dipped into black ink made of lampblack (a kind of soot) and natural gum.

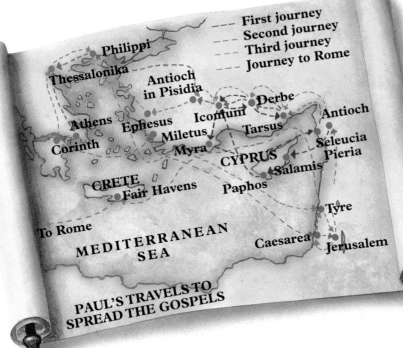

First journey
Second journey
Third journey
Journey to Rome

Philippi
Thessalonika
Antioch in Pisidia
Athens
Ephesus
Iconium
Derbe
Antioch
Corinth
Miletus
Tarsus
Myra
Seleucia Pieria
CYPRUS
Salamis
CRETE
Fair Havens
Paphos
Tyre
To Rome
MEDITERRANEAN SEA
Caesarea
Jerusalem

PAUL'S TRAVELS TO SPREAD THE GOSPELS

The Dead Sea scrolls

In 1947 a young Bedouin goat-herd made a remarkable discovery. In caves high above the Dead Sea, he found several old pottery jars. In them were ancient scrolls. They turned out to be scriptures and historical records that may have been copied down in the nearby Jewish community of Qumran. Among them were the oldest known copies of various books of the Old Testament of the Bible.

A fragment of a scroll found at Qumran

▼ *The story of the Jews and the teachings of Christ are recorded in the Bible, which consists of 66 books. These stories were written and copied down over hundreds of years.*

Most of the scriptures were written on parchment – very thin sheets of sheep or goat skin – and made into scrolls.

Scribes were people whose job it was to write. Most people could not write, so they paid scribes to write letters and other documents for them.

All roads lead to Rome

The Romans believed that straight roads were essential for running their huge empire. The roads were carefully constructed in several layers, which varied according to the materials found nearby. Messengers could carry orders swiftly along these roads and soldiers could march quickly along them. All parts of the Roman empire were linked by the network of roads and shipping routes that spread out from the capital, Rome. It was along roads like this that Christianity spread from the Bible lands and into the world beyond.

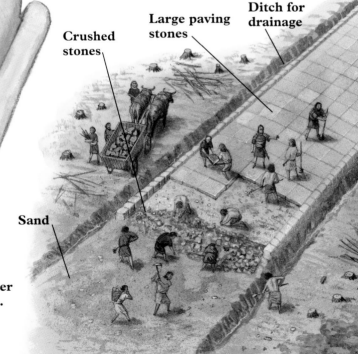

Ditch for drainage

Large paving stones

Crushed stones

Sand

27

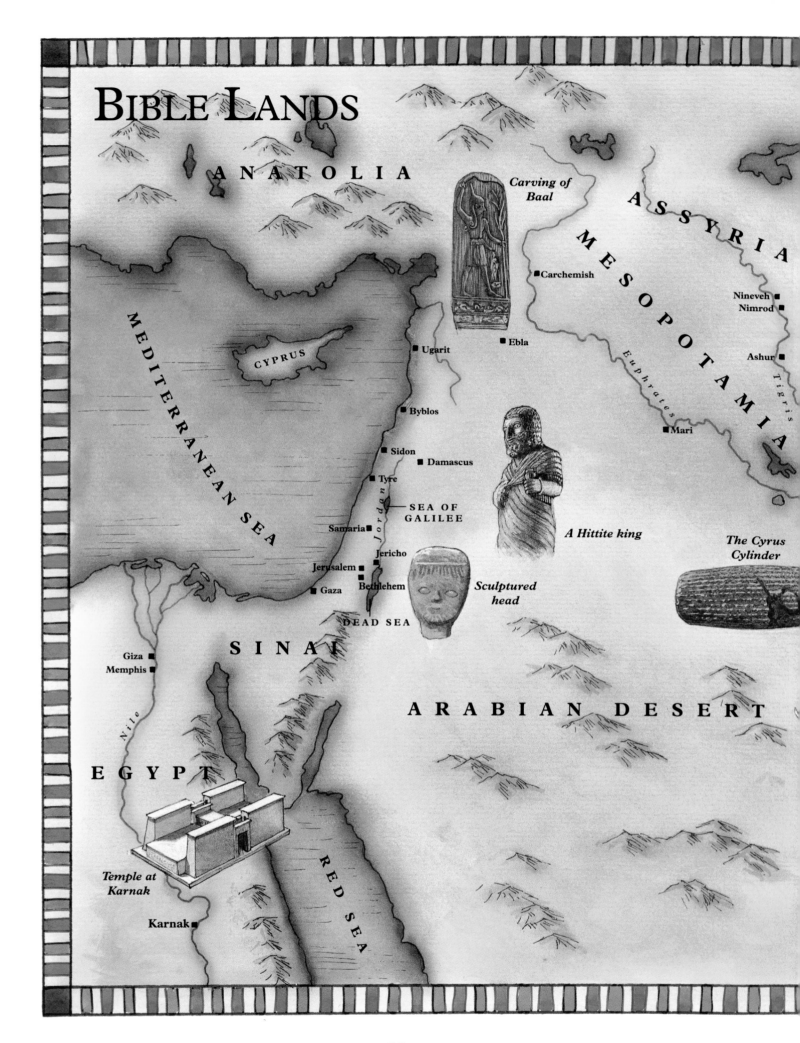

BIBLE LANDS

ANATOLIA

ASSYRIA

MESOPOTAMIA

Carving of Baal

Carchemish

Nineveh
Nimrod

Ashur

CYPRUS

Ugarit

Ebla

Mari

MEDITERRANEAN SEA

Byblos

Sidon

Damascus

Tyre

A Hittite king

The Cyrus Cylinder

SEA OF GALILEE

Samaria

Jericho

Jerusalem

Bethlehem

Gaza

Sculptured head

DEAD SEA

SINAI

Giza
Memphis

ARABIAN DESERT

EGYPT

Temple at Karnak

Karnak

RED SEA

Nile

Euphrates

Tigris

Jordan

INDEX

Black obelisk from Nimrod

Decorated figure of a goat from Ur

SEARCH FOR THE SCRIPTURES

If you've ever wanted to search for ancient treasures, here's your chance. On the way you can travel through Biblical lands and see a towering ziggurat, visit Herod's palace or ride on a camel with nomads. As an amateur archaeologist, you need to be on the lookout for precious ancient scriptures to collect and take to the museum. The first one to reach the museum wins!

RULES

1. This is a game for two to four players. You need to supply your own dice to play the game or use the template in the book to make your own spinner (see instructions bottom right). You will also need different coloured buttons to use as counters.

2. Each player throws the dice in turn to move his or her counter. The aim is to collect scrolls (S), tablets (T), and cuneiform seals (C). To do this, a player must land on a space with a picture of the relevant scripture. Use counters of different colours to represent the different scriptures (for example; yellow for cuneiform, red for tablets and so on). Don't forget that the counters used as the scriptures must be different colours than those used as counters.

3. On the way there are spaces with instructions on them. Some of these help the collector, for example, "take a scroll from any player" and some hinder the collector, for example, "visit a pyramid: miss a turn".

4. Each player has to collect one of each type of scripture: a scroll, a tablet and a cuneiform seal. When a player has collected all three scriptures, it is time to take them to the museum in the centre of the board. To do this the player goes to the red squares and then follows the red path to the museum in the middle. To win the game the player has to throw the exact number to land on the museum space.

Enjoy the search and good luck!

Copy the template onto a piece of thin cardboard. Cut it out and make a hole in the center. Push a toothpick through the hole and your spinner is ready to use.